Toni Morrison

Corinne J. Naden and Rose Blue

Chicago, Illinois

© 2006 Raintree
Published by Raintree, a division of Reed Elsevier, Inc.
Chicago, Illinois
Customer Service: 888-363-4266
Visit our website at www.raintreelibrary.com

All rights reserved. No part of this book may be reproduced or transmitted in any form or by any means, electronic or mechanical, including photocopying, recording, taping, or any information storage and retrieval system, without permission in writing from the publisher.

For information, address the publisher:
Raintree, 100 N. LaSalle, Suite 1200, Chicago, IL 60602

Photo research by Bill Broyles

Printed and bound in China by South China Printing Company.
10 09 08 07 06
10 9 8 7 6 5 4 3 2 1

Library of Congress Cataloging-in-Publication Data:

Naden, Corinne J.
  Toni Morrison / Corinne J. Naden and Rose Blue.
    p. cm. -- (African-American biographies)
  Includes bibliographical references and index.
  ISBN 1-4109-1043-1 (hc) 1-4109-1120-9 (pb)
  1. Morrison, Toni--Juvenile literature. 2. Novelists, American--20th century--Biography--Juvenile literature. 3. African American novelists--Biography--Juvenile literature. I. Blue, Rose. II. Title. III. Series: African American biographies (Chicago, Ill.)
  PS3563.O8749Z785 2005
  813'.54--dc22
                        2005004825

Acknowledgments
The publisher would like to thank the following for permission to reproduce photographs:
p. 4 James Keyser/Time Life Pictures/Getty Images; pp. 8, 27 Corbis; p. 11 Spanky's Yearbook Archive; p. 13 Black River Historical Society; p. 18 Alfred Eisenstaedt/Time Life Pictures/Getty Images; pp. 21, 22, 51 Bettmann/Corbis; p. 24 Texas Southern University; p. 29 AP Wide World Photo; p. 32 Paul Almasy/Corbis; p. 36 Plume Books; p. 38 Knopf; p. 41 Evan Agostini/Getty Images; p. 44 Paul Rocheleau/Index Stock Imagery; p. 48 Bernard Gotfryd/Hulton Archive/Getty Images; p. 52 David Bookstaver/AP Wide World Photo; p. 54 Corbis Sygma; p. 56 Robert Maas/Corbis; p. 59 Nancy Kaszerman/Zuma/Corbis

Cover photograph: by Nancy Kaszerman/Zuma/Corbis

Every effort has been made to contact copyright holders of any material reproduced in this book. Any omissions will be rectified in subsequent printings if notice is given to the publisher

Some words are shown in bold, **like this**. You can find out what they mean by looking in the Glossary.

Contents

Introduction: The Highest Honor 5

Chapter 1: Growing Up in Ohio 9

Chapter 2: New Experiences 19

Chapter 3: Morrison Becomes a Writer 33

Chapter 4: The Novelist in the City 39

Chapter 5: Success! 45

Chapter 6: Reaching the Top 53

Glossary 60

Timeline 62

Further Information 63

Index 64

Toni Morrison is shown here in a photo taken at her home. Among her numerous awards are honorary degrees from more than fifteen universities. Honorary degrees are awards of recognition given by colleges and universities.

Introduction: The Highest Honor

On Tuesday afternoon, December 7, 1993, Toni Morrison stood before an audience at the Swedish Academy in Stockholm, Sweden. Dressed in a black gown, she began her speech with the words "Once upon a time." She was giving her acceptance speech for receiving the Nobel Prize in **Literature**, considered by many to be a writer's highest honor. She was the first African-American woman and only the eighth woman ever to be so honored in literature.

The Nobel Prize was not the first award Morrison won for her work. She has received the Pulitzer Prize for fiction, the National Book Critics Circle award, the American Academy and Institute of Arts and Letters award, and the National Book Foundation Medal for Distinguished Contribution to American Letters, among others.

In Her Own Words

"If there's a book you really want to read, but it hasn't been written yet, then you must write it."

"The ability of writers to imagine what is not the self, to familiarize the strange and mystify the familiar, is the test of their power."

"There is really nothing more to say—except why. But since why is difficult to handle, one must take refuge in how."

"When there is pain, there are no words. All pain is the same."

I'm a Midwesterner, and everyone in Ohio is excited. I'm also a New Yorker, and a New Jerseyan, and an American, plus I'm an African American, and a woman. . . . I'd like to think of the prize being distributed to these regions and nations and races. *(from her Nobel Prize acceptance speech)*

Toni Morrison is a gifted storyteller. She often writes of troubled characters that are trying to find themselves in a society that is not always kind. She writes about what she knows, about her childhood experiences. She writes about love and hate and what these emotions can do to people. She writes about race and about what **injustice** does to everyone, no matter what race or color they may be. But most of all, Toni Morrison writes about life.

Morrison's grandparents worked as sharecroppers. These sharecroppers worked in cotton fields in Georgia in the late 1800s.

Chapter 1:
Growing Up in Ohio

Toni Morrison was born Chloe Anthony Wofford on February 18, 1931, the second of four children. She was born in the small midwestern town of Lorain, Ohio, but to understand her childhood, it is important to understand where her family came from.

Chloe's grandparents had been slaves. After the Civil War ended in 1865, slavery in Southern states became illegal, but the former slaves had nowhere to live or work. Like many former slaves, Chloe's grandparents became **sharecroppers**. Her mother's parents were sharecroppers in Kentucky and her father's parents were sharecroppers in Alabama.

As sharecroppers, former slaves lived on and farmed land owned by white people—sometimes their former masters. The sharecroppers were paid for the crops they raised, but most of that money went to the landowners to pay for housing and farming supplies. **Sharecropping** was not a fair system. Many landowners paid the sharecroppers less than they were owed, so the sharecroppers could not afford to pay for their homes. As a result, the sharecroppers owed the landowners money, and they usually could not make enough to pay the landowners back. If the sharecroppers complained about how unfair this was, they were often arrested.

At this time, there were many laws in the South that were extremely unfair to African Americans. For example, black people were not allowed to vote. The South was also **segregated**. African Americans and white Americans could not sit in the same railroad cars, use the same drinking fountains, or even play checkers together. Both sets of Chloe's grandparents left the South in search of a better life in the North.

Chloe's mother's parents moved to Ohio when Chloe's mother, Ramah, was very young. Chloe's grandfather, John Solomon Willis, sometimes found extra work playing the violin. Once he got a musician's job far from home, so he had to move away for a while. Chloe's grandmother was afraid of living alone with her small children in the South. She had only $18 in her pocket, but she decided the family had to move north. She sent her husband a message about her decision, hoping he would receive it before she decided to leave. When the time came, she and the children got on a train that left at midnight. They were thrilled to find Chloe's

This photo was featured in Morrison's 1949 high-school yearbook. She worked as a librarian's aide in high school.

grandfather on the train, too. That is how their family came to Lorain, Ohio.

Chloe's mother grew up in the North and didn't experience the same degree of **prejudice** her parents experienced, but **racism** still existed. Chloe's father, George, on the other hand, was raised in Alabama. As a boy, white people treated him poorly and he never forgot that. The year his family left Alabama, three African-American men in their community were **lynched**. As a result of his childhood experiences, George came to distrust and hate all white people. He thought there was something wrong with white people who treated him poorly. Even as an adult living in Ohio, Chloe's father would not let white people inside his house.

Chloe's mother had a different way of dealing with the way some white people treated African Americans. She was a very religious woman who thought the best way to bring people together was to educate them and point out what they were doing wrong. Chloe's mother tried to prevent Lorain from becoming a **segregated** town. When a new business opened up in town, she would visit the business. If it seemed like the business had a separate section for black people and a separate section for white people, she would complain to the manager. She would do this every day until she was sure that African-American customers could use the business in the same manner that white people could.

This photo shows downtown Lorain, Ohio, Morrison's hometown, in about 1935.

Laughter and music

Despite their hardships, lots of love and laughter filled the Wofford home. Chloe's mother sang jazz and **opera** and played the piano. Her grandparents told her stories about slavery and how poor they had been as **sharecroppers**.

Besides the family history, there was much magic and a great sense of the spiritual world in the tales Chloe's grandparents told. They often spoke of ghosts and **myths** and dreams.

At a very early age, Chloe learned to love books. Grandfather Willis was a great reader, though he had been to school only one day in his life. Her mother belonged to a book club even though the family had little money. She taught Chloe that books were treasures. By the time Chloe started the first grade, she was the only child in the class who could read.

In Her Own Words

"My grandfather went to school for one day—to tell the teacher he would not be back. Yet all his adult life he read greedily, as did his uneducated friends."

A diverse neighborhood

All kinds of people lived in Chloe's neighborhood. An Italian family lived on one side of the Woffords and a Greek family on the other. Lorain was too small and everyone was too poor to worry about who their neighbors were. Even so, there were places in Lorain that black people were not welcome. One of them was the town park. Part of Lake Erie was in the park, but only white kids could swim there.

Her school was **racially** mixed, too. In first grade she was the only African-American student in her class. In general, she did not feel threatened because of her skin color, and most of her friends were white. But once in a while older boys would throw rocks at her and her friends and call them names. Once, when Chloe was in fifth grade, a new student came to her class. He didn't speak English, but he sat next to Chloe and she taught him how to read. Because he wasn't from the United States originally, he had no real understanding of the struggles between black people and white people. It took him six months to realize that Chloe was black, and when he did, he insulted her and did not speak to her anymore.

When Chloe was thirteen, she had to help bring money into the house. She had many jobs, including cleaning a house for a white family. One day she complained to her father that the work was too hard and the people were mean. He told her to remember that she did not live in the house. She just worked there. Do the work, get the money, and come home, he said.

An honor student

Chloe grew up feeling secure in her family and in her neighborhood. Everyone seemed to watch out for one another. She was a very good student. By the time she was in high school, she was reading famous American writers such as Ernest Hemingway and Willa Cather. She also read Russian and French works and novels by the 19th-century English writer Jane Austen. But she never thought of becoming a writer herself. Instead, she very much wanted to be a great ballerina. Her **idol** was the famous star of the New York City Ballet, Maria Tallchief.

Chloe was a member of the National Honor Society while in high school, and she served on the student council. She graduated from Lorain High School with honors in 1949. Even though her family was very poor, she wanted to go on to college. No woman, and just one man, in her family had ever gone to college.

She applied to and was accepted at Howard University in Washington, D.C. It was founded in 1867 as a school for African Americans. But Howard has always been open to those of any race or color. Many famous black Americans graduated from Howard, such as Supreme Court Justice Thurgood Marshall, actor Ossie Davis, and **opera** singer Jessye Norman. Howard is one of the most respected colleges in the United States.

Chloe was happy to leave Lorain as a seventeen-year-old high school graduate. She thought she was ready to leave her small town and see the world. By working three jobs, her father had managed to put some money away for her education. Her mother also took a part-time job. In 1949 Chloe Anthony Wofford left Ohio for Howard University.

This photo shows Howard University in about 1950. Founders Library, a campus landmark, can be seen in the background.

Chapter 2:
New Experiences

Chloe chose Howard University because she thought it would be full of "brilliant black students." Howard was considered the center of educated African-American life in the United States. She thought she would meet people smarter than she was and learn amazing things from them. Chloe majored in English and minored in classic **literature**, thinking she would learn about black **culture** by studying the works of African-American writers. However, she was disappointed. Chloe soon learned that Howard students were pretty much like college students anywhere. Her new friends were more interested in clothes and parties and being "cool" than education.

As for studying African-American writers, Chloe's classes were mainly about literature written by white writers such as William Shakespeare. In the early 1950s students spent little time studying African-American writers—even at Howard. When Chloe suggested

Howard University

When the Civil War ended in 1865, there were four million newly freed slaves with little or no education and no job skills. In November 1866, a group of ministers and abolitionists (people who were against slavery) convinced the United States Congress to open a school to train former slaves to become ministers. The Howard Normal and Theological Institute for the Education of Preachers and Teachers opened its doors the following year. It was named for Oliver Howard, a general in the Civil War and one of the school's founders. The name was soon changed to Howard University, and classes were offered in many different subjects. Always open to all races, Howard's first students were four white women.

Today, Howard has more than 10,000 students from a variety of backgrounds.

writing a report about the black characters in Shakespeare's plays, her professor discouraged her from doing so.

Living in Washington D.C. was also a shock for Chloe. Black people and white people were **segregated** in Washington, but there was also a level of segregation in the black community. African-Americans with lighter skin were considered superior to African-Americans with darker skin. There was even something

The Capitol building can be seen in this photo of a Washington, D.C. street in about 1950.

Morrison was surprised about the degree of segregation that she witnessed in Washington, D.C. and in the South.

known as the "paper bag test." Some establishments did not allow black people whose skin was darker than a brown paper bag. "I was so ignorant about the world," Morrison later said about this experience.

While at Howard, Chloe (who now called herself "Toni," a shortened version of Anthony, her middle name) joined a theatrical group called the Howard University Players. She thought this might be one place where hard work and talent really mattered.

The theatrical group had been created in 1907 by a group of Howard students who performed the plays of Shakespeare on campus and around Washington, D.C. At that time, the company was called the College Dramatic Club. The hope was that the group would some day establish an African-American theater to showcase the talents of African-American performers everywhere. By 1925, the group had changed its name to the Howard University Players. The Players had earned a reputation for performing plays that told of African-American life and for producing terrific actors.

As a member of the Howard University Players, Toni appeared in many campus productions. When the company toured the South, Toni got a firsthand look the kind of **racism** her grandparents had known. All through her childhood, Toni had heard so much about what life was like for African-American people, but she never really understood it. On the tour, the actors performed for completely **segregated** audiences. What Toni saw and experienced in the South later worked its way into her novels.

In 1953 Toni graduated from Howard University. She decided to continue her education at Cornell University in Ithaca, New York. After finding college to be fairly easy, Toni was surprised at

This photo shows Texas Southern University, where Morrison taught English, in 1967.

how hard the work was at Cornell. She spent many long hours in the library. For her graduation **thesis**, she wrote about the works of William Faulkner and Virginia Woolf. In 1955 she earned a master's degree in English. Now she was ready to begin a career. She just had to decide what it was.

Morrison had not really planned to become a teacher, but now it seemed like a good idea. She was offered a position at Texas Southern University (also an historically black college) in Houston to teach introductory English. Much to her delight, she really enjoyed teaching **undergraduates**. She was also delighted with the college itself. Texas Southern had a different idea about how to teach black students than Howard had. At the time, Howard University's approach was to give its students the same educational experiences students at white universities had. At Texas Southern, there was more of a focus on teaching students about African-American **culture and literature** and the important contributions made by African Americans throughout history. The college even dedicated a week to celebrating black history, something Morrison had never experienced before.

During her two years at Texas Southern University, Morrison began to think seriously about what it meant to be African-American in the United States. She began to believe that African-American culture was something that should be taught and studied.

A time of change

In 1957 Toni returned to Howard University and became an instructor in English. Howard was a different place than it had been during her **undergraduate** years. In fact, the whole country was different. The modern **civil rights** movement had just begun.

In the South, African Americans were beginning to protest **segregation** and the fact that their rights were not protected by the Constitution of the United States. For example, in the South for most of the 20th century, black children and white children could not go to school together. In 1954 the Supreme Court, the most powerful court in the United States, declared that the segregation of public schools was illegal.

The next year, a woman named Rosa Parks refused to give up her seat on a Montgomery, Alabama bus to a white passenger. At the time, African Americans were only allowed to sit at the backs of buses, and if a bus was full, African-American passengers had to give up their seats to let white passengers sit down. Even though she knew the rules, Parks had worked a long, hard day and needed a rest. She thought she deserved to sit down. When she did not stand so a white person could sit down, she was arrested.

In protest, Montgomery's black community refused to ride the city buses. Thousands of African Americans walked to work for more than a year. People all over the country watched as the

One of the most famous marches staged to bring attention to the civil rights movement became known as the March on Washington. About 250,000 people attended the march and listened to speeches in Washington, D.C., in August 1963.

protest went on. Many of them were especially impressed with the man who lead the boycott—Dr. Martin Luther King Jr. In 1956 the buses were **desegregated** and the boycott ended.

In reaction to the growing **civil rights** movement, teachers and students at Howard demanded more classes that focused on African-American **culture**. Howard had become the university Toni had wanted it to be when she was a student there.

While at Howard, Toni met many people who would later become key players in the fight for civil rights. One of her students was Stokely Carmichael. He would later become head of the Student Nonviolent Coordinating Committee (SNCC) and a leader in the Black Power movement. She also met Andrew Young, who would join Dr. King in nonviolent protests and would later become mayor of Atlanta, Georgia. Toni also met a poet named LeRoi Jones. Writing poetry under the name Amiri Baraka, Jones was outspoken in the fight for social **justice**.

While Toni was interested in the struggle for civil rights, she did not take an active part in the fight. Instead, she concentrated on her teaching and fell in love. In 1958 she married a Jamaican architect named Harold Morrison. In 1961 they had their first son, Harold Ford.

Stokely Carmichael, one of Morrison's students at Howard University, appeared on the television show Face the Nation *in the 1960s.*

Stokely Carmichael

Stokely Carmichael was born in Port of Spain, Trinidad, on June 29, 1941. When he was two years old, his family moved to New York City.

In 1960 Carmichael enrolled at Howard University, where he majored in **philosophy**. At Howard, Carmichael became very involved in the **civil rights** movement. When he graduated in 1964, he focused his energy on fighting **segregation** in the South through nonviolent protests. Seeing the violent attacks of **racist** Southern groups against black protesters, however, made Carmichael believe that nonviolence was not the answer. Black people needed to fight racism any way they could.

In 1965 Carmichael began to call for "black power," meaning that black people had the power to vote for politicians who would take care of their needs. Unfortunately, many people thought that "black power" was a cry for an African-American revolution.

Frustrated with the United States, Carmichael moved to New Guinea, a country in Africa in 1969. Except for a few visits, he stayed away from the U.S. until the 1990s. By then he had changed his name to Kwame Ture. Ture died on November 15, 1996, still believing the U.S. has a long way to go in the fight against racism.

Soon after her son was born, Toni joined a writers' group at Howard. She joined the group to help her forget how troubled her marriage had become. There were ten writers in the group. They met once a month to read and discuss each other's work. Every month, each member had to bring something he or she had written. Toni brought stories that she had written in high school to the meetings. When she ran out of high-school stories, she wrote a tale about a little black girl whose greatest wish was to have blue eyes. The other writers really liked the story. Toni was pleased with their comments, but she did not work on the story further.

In 1964 Toni left her teaching position at Howard. She went to Europe for the summer with her husband and son. Even though Toni was expecting their second child, she and her husband were not getting along. They separated while in Europe and they eventually divorced.

Toni Morrison was now 34 years old with no job, a small son to support, and another child about to be born. She decided to go home to Ohio and to her family. Her second son, Slade Kevin, was born there.

Toni knew that she could stay in Lorain and that her family would help her raise her two sons. But she wanted to live her own life. She wanted to find out if she was strong enough to make it on her own.

Morrison worked in New York City in the 1970s. Midtown Manhattan is shown in this photo from the 1970s. The Empire State Building can be seen in the middle of the photo.

Chapter 3:
Morrison Becomes a Writer

In 1965 Toni Morrison saw an ad in *The New York Review of Books*. A textbook company, part of Random House publishers, in Syracuse, New York, needed to hire an editor. She thought that publishing could be the start of a new career.

Toni applied for the job and was hired as an associate editor. She and her two small sons moved to Syracuse. In Syracuse, life was very lonely for her. She knew no one. A housekeeper took care of the children during the day while she worked. At night, she returned home to cook dinner for the boys and put them to bed.

The winters were long, cold, and snowy in Syracuse. To help ease her loneliness, Toni began to write at night after the children were asleep. That first winter, she took out the story about the little black girl who wanted blue eyes. She filled her lonely nights by turning the story into a novel. The more she wrote, the more important writing became to her. It helped lift her out of her loneliness. Morrison later said that at that point she knew she was "never going to stop writing—that was what I was about."

In New York City

In 1967, after eighteen months in Syracuse, Toni was transferred to Random House headquarters in New York City. In her new job, she worked on books that would be found in bookstores all over the United States.

Now a senior editor, Morrison took a special interest in books by African-American authors. She became passionate about helping them tell their stories. At Random House, Morrison edited about six or seven books a year. Two of the best were the autobiographies of famous boxer Muhammad Ali and of **civil rights activist** Angela Davis. But Toni never told anyone at Random House about her own novel. She had written three-fourths of it by then.

She sent her unfinished work to an editor at Holt, Rinehart, and Winston, another publishing company in New York. The editor who read it told her to finish the book. She would wake up early in the morning, before her children were awake, to write. On the train ride to work, she would figure out parts of the story in her head, then jot them down when she got to her office.

When she finished her book, the editor at Holt, Rinehart, and Winston accepted her novel for publication. *The Bluest Eye* was published in 1970. Toni's career as a published author had begun.

The reaction

Toni Morrison's first novel did not sell many copies when it was first published. However, it was reviewed in many well-known publications. The critics said it was an impressive first novel. They said her use of language had the smooth flow of poetry.

The Bluest Eye

The Bluest Eye is about eleven-year-old Pecola Breedlove, an African-American girl growing up in a small, Midwestern town in the early 1940s. Abused by both of her parents, Pecola feels unloved and ugly because she is black. She focuses all of her attention on her doll made to look like Shirley Temple, a white child actress from the 1940s. Shirley Temple, with her blond hair and blue eyes, was known as America's Sweetheart. Pecola believes that if she had blue eyes, she would be loved and her life would become perfect. She prays desperately for the bluest eyes possible. By the end of the book, so many tragic things happen to Pecola that she goes insane. She believes that she truly has been given the bluest eyes.

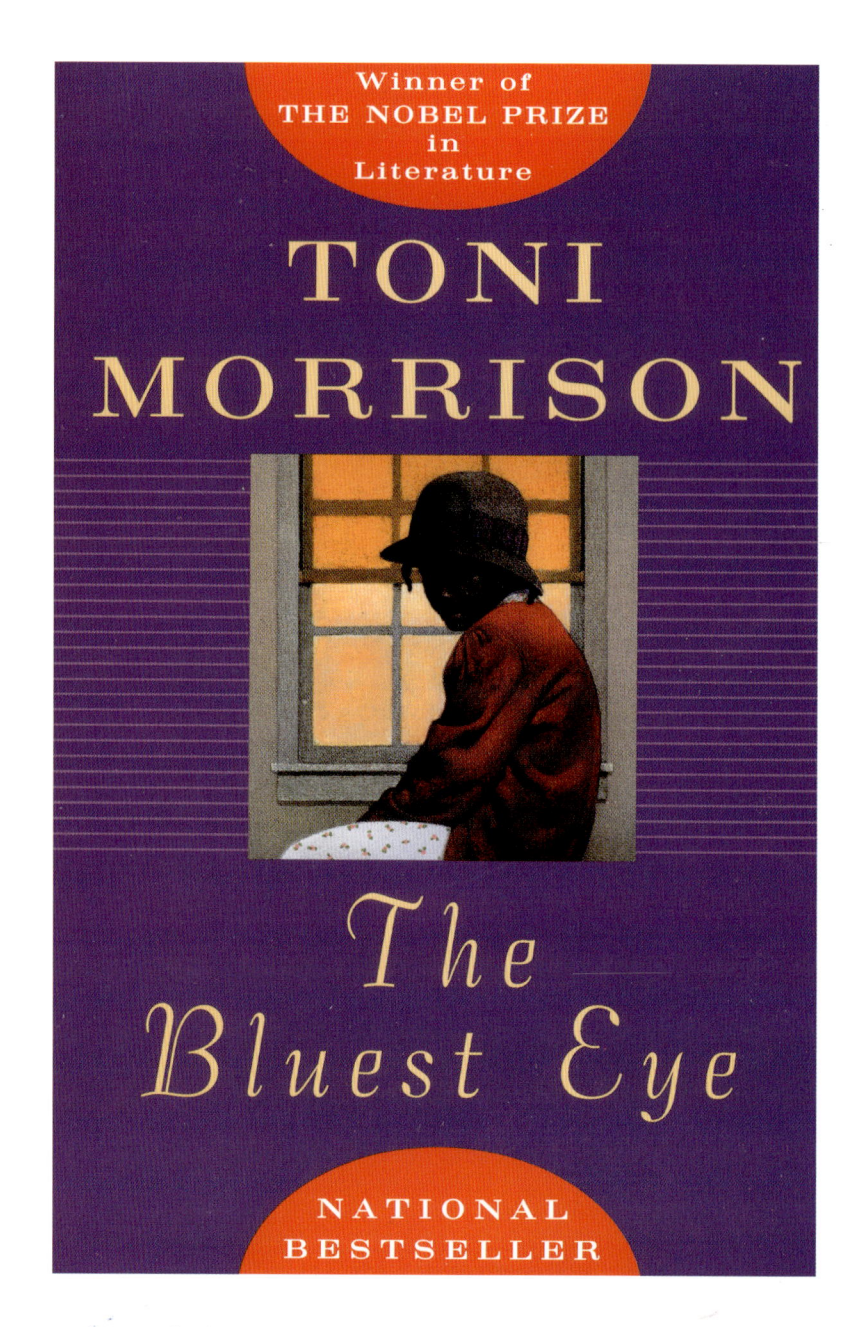

Morrison came up with the story of The Bluest Eye, *her first published book, in the early 1960s.*

At first, Toni was upset when she saw the published book. She had meant to use the name she was born with, Chloe Wofford, on the cover. But in all the excitement, she forgot to tell the editor. From now on, the reading world would know her as Toni Morrison.

The Bluest Eye was a great success because it began her career as an important American novelist. During the writing of it, Toni began to realize what her true work was going to be. She did not yet see herself as a novelist, even when the book was published. In fact, for the next few months, she did very little writing. But then a new character began to take shape in her mind. Soon there was an idea for another novel.

In Her Own Words

"All the women I knew did nine or ten things at one time. I always understood that women worked, they went to church, they managed their houses, they managed somebody else's houses, they raised their children, they raised somebody else's children, they taught. I wouldn't say it's not hard, but why wouldn't it be? All important things are hard."

Sula, *Morrison's second novel, was published in 1973. It told the story of two African-American women growing up in the town of Medallion, Ohio.*

Chapter 4:
The Novelist in the City

Morrison began writing her second novel in her head while riding the subway to and from work. As she had before, she would put her ideas down on paper when she got home or to the office. At home, she tried to write in a room away from her sons so that she could concentrate. But her sons kept coming to her wanting to play or with questions. Soon she moved her writing to the kitchen table where her sons could be near her. Despite the noise, she found she could concentrate, and her boys were happy just because she was there.

While writing her second novel, Morrison took a second job, teaching English at the State University of New York (SUNY). She still worked as an editor for Random House. She did not have time for anything else but work, her sons, and her writing. She was still most productive in the early mornings, but she also wrote over the summers while her children were with her parents in Lorain. Anytime she could grab a moment, she would write.

Sula

Morrison's second novel, *Sula*, took her two and a half years to write. It was published in late 1973. She dedicated the book to her sons, who were twelve and eight years old at the time.

At the heart of *Sula* is the powerful friendship between two girls—Sula and Nel. They are inseparable until a tragic accident causes them to drift apart. After high school, Nel gets married and settles into life as a wife and mother. Sula, on the other hand, leaves home and has wild adventures. When she returns ten years later, the townspeople believe that the things she has done and seen made her evil. Sula and Nel still have a bit of their friendship left, but Sula soon destroys it. Soon everyone in town hates Sula. In a strange way, this brings the townspeople together and helps them get along. When Sula dies, however, the closeness the townspeople shared disappears.

Sula was nominated for the National Book Award for fiction in 1975. Most critics praised the book, especially for its interesting characters. But some reviewers were not so pleased. They did not like the attitude of the townspeople in the book, who did nothing to stop Sula's terrible behavior. Toni responded by saying that the critics did not understand African-American **culture.** According to

As her writing career blossomed, Morrison was frequently asked to speak at events and give lectures about writing.

Morrison, there was a time when black people thought evil had a natural place in life. They chose to protect themselves from evil, not destroy it.

Like *The Bluest Eye*, Toni's second novel did not bring in much money at first. But it did expand her reputation as a talented novelist. She was frequently asked to give lectures. She was in great demand at colleges and universities, especially those that offered classes in African-American history and **culture**. With just two novels, Toni was becoming known as a writer who understood the values, customs, and feelings of African Americans.

Even with the publication of *Sula* and *The Bluest Eye*, Morrison was still an editor at Random House. As an editor, she turned her attention to a project that was close to her heart. *The Black Book*, a collection of African-American history from slavery to modern times, published by Random House in 1974. *The Black Book* included newspaper clippings, faded photographs, old song lyrics, slave quilts, and many other treasures from the past. Morrison also contributed items from her own family. It showed 300 years of rich African-American history as told by the people who lived it. *The Black Book* was Toni's idea, but her name does not appear on the finished project.

After her second novel and her work on *The Black Book*, Morrison was busier than ever. During this period, she and her sons moved to Spring Valley, New York, about an hour's drive from New York City. In the morning, she drove her sons to school by 8:00 in the morning before going to work at Random House. At 3:30 in the afternoon, she picked them up again and headed home.

Morrison agreed to teach one day a week—on Fridays—at Yale University in Connecticut. She was a visiting professor for the 1976–1977 school year. She taught classes on the writings of African-American women and on the technique of writing fiction.

With editing, teaching, and raising her sons, Morrison did not seem to have time for anything else. But another idea was forming in her mind. It would become her third novel. Sadly, as she was working on it, her beloved father died.

Morrison was a visiting professor at Yale University in New Haven, Connecticut, for the 1976–1977 school year.

Chapter 5: Success!

Morrison found it very difficult to continue writing after the death of her father. She said later that she often had long conversations with him in her head. Her third book, *Song of Solomon*, is dedicated to him with just one word: "Daddy."

Song of Solomon

Song of Solomon, published in 1977, is the story of a boy named Milkman. He goes on a journey from his Michigan home to find out about his past. In Virginia, Milkman uncovers his family history, including information about his great grandfather, Solomon, who was a slave. According to legend, to escape slavery, Solomon "flew" back to Africa. This idea is based on a folktale first told by African slaves about flying to freedom. In the book, Morrison explains that slaves may have begun to tell the flying tales as a way of escape their misery and find hope in their lives.

The Myth of the Flying Africans

"The **Myth** of the Flying Africans," which inspired Toni Morrison's book *Song of Solomon,* has been told and retold for generations. It is part of the oral tradition of African-American **culture**. Oral traditions are bits of history told by one generation to the next in story or song. For many years, the stories and songs were not written down. Each person telling a story or singing a song did it a little differently, so the stories and songs changed over the years. But the basic ideas stayed the same.

Historians think the myth of the flying Africans is based on an actual event that happened off the coast of Georgia in 1803. A group of Africans, members of the Igbo tribe from what is now Nigeria, were forced aboard a ship heading for Savannah, Georgia. The Igbo took control of the ship, defeating their white captors. When the boat arrived in Savannah, witnesses saw the Igbo walk from the ship and into the water where they drowned. When other slaves heard the story, they began to imagine that the Igbo rose into the sky and flew back to Africa—to freedom.

There are many versions of the Myth of the Flying Africans, but each one has the common idea of hope that someday, somehow, the slaves would be free.

Song of Solomon was different for Morrison because it focused on men instead of women. She admitted that it was difficult at first for her to write from a man's point of view, but she learned a lot by watching her two growing sons.

With the publication of *Song of Solomon*, Morrison became an established, respected writer. And for the first time, one of her novels sold well. She remembers being especially thrilled when she saw a sign in a bookstore that read "A Triumph by Toni Morrison."

Song of Solomon won many honors. It was a Book-of-the-Month Club selection. The Book-of-the-Month Club began in 1926 as a way to help people across the United States choose the books they should read. Morrison was the first African-American author to have a book chosen as a book of the month since 1940. *Song of Solomon* also received the National Book Critics Circle Award and recognition from the American Academy and Institute of Arts and Letters. The book was a bestseller in both hardcover and paperback.

With the success of *Song of Solomon,* Morrison finally felt ready to make writing her career. She left Random House, and with the money she earned from her books, bought a houseboat about an hour's drive from New York City. The houseboat was located right on the Hudson River, so she could sit on her large porch in a swing and look out over the water. Her sons transferred to a nearby school. She began to plan her fourth novel.

This photo of Morrison was taken at her home. Song of Solomon was not the only one of Morrison's books that was chosen for a book club. Oprah Winfrey later chose three other Morrison books for her book club.

Tar Baby

Tar Baby, Morrison's fourth novel, was published in 1981. It took more than four years for her to complete it. *Tar Baby* is the story of Jadine, a beautiful model who went to school in Europe, and Son, a man who was raised in a small town in Florida. Although they fall in love, their different backgrounds make their relationship very difficult.

Tar Baby got book reviewers' attention and Morrison became sought after by the press. She laughed when she heard that *Newsweek* magazine was going to put her on the cover of their March 30, 1981 issue. She said could not imagine that the magazine wanted a "middle-aged, gray-haired, colored woman." But *Newsweek* did, and Morrison became one of the first African-American women in the magazine's history to receive that honor. She was featured in many other magazines and newspapers around the country as well.

Tar Baby was a great success for Morrison. It remained on the bestseller list for four months. But not all the critics liked it. Some said the plot was too complicated. Others said that she was not as skilled at writing about white people as she was at writing about African Americans. But most readers thought *Tar Baby* was a fine novel that put Toni Morrison high up on the list of great American writers.

American writers.

Busier than before

Morrison went on a nationwide tour to promote the book, visiting fourteen cities. During this time, she became more outspoken about public issues. At a meeting of the National Council on the Arts, she spoke against cuts in programs for the arts by then-president Ronald Reagan.

In 1983 Toni left her part-time editing position at Random House after twenty years. The following year, she became the Albert Schweitzer Professor of the Humanities at the State University of New York in Albany. Her job was to help young writers.

In addition to her teaching, Toni took time out to write her first play in 1986. It was called *Dreaming Emmett* and based on a true story of a fourteen-year-old African-American boy from Chicago who went to visit relatives in Mississippi in the summer of 1955. Because he spoke to a white woman in a store, he was kidnapped and killed by white **racists** and thrown in the river.

In *Dreaming Emmett*, the boy comes back from the dead and talks about what happened to him. Toni spoke of it as a play about imagination. People who read it spoke very highly of the play. Critics praised it, too. It won the New York State Governor's Art Award.

Emmett Till

In the Summer of 1955, fourteen-year-old Emmett Till and his cousin Curtis Jones traveled from Chicago (Emmett's hometown) to Mississippi to visit family. Before Emmett left, his mother warned him that Mississippi was a dangerous place for black people. The Ku Klux Klan, a racist group that terrorized African-Americans, was very powerful. Emmett's mother kissed her son good-bye and gave him a ring that had once belonged to his father.

On August 24, Emmett and Curtis went to Bryant's Grocery Store to buy some candy. Some local boys dared Emmett to talk to Carolyn Bryant, the store clerk and the wife of the store's white owner. Emmett went inside, bought some candy, and, according to reports, whistled at Carolyn Bryant.

Four days later, Roy Bryant (Carolyn's husband) and another man dragged Emmett from his bed and disappeared with him. Three days later, Emmett's body was found in a river. He'd been beaten and shot. His face was so damaged that the only way he could be identified was by the ring his mother had given him.

Toni Morrison is pictured here promoting her book, Beloved. *Authors frequently go on book tours to promote, or increase the sales of, new books after they are first published.*

Chapter 6:
Reaching the Top

For some time, long before working on her play, Morrison was planning her fifth novel in her head. It was published in 1987 and was a novel about slavery. Many critics have said it is her finest work.

Beloved

Beloved is a story of memories. Morrison got the idea for the book after reading a story she had discovered while editing *The Black Book*. It was the story of Margaret Garner, a runaway slave who, about to be captured, killed her child so the child would not be returned to slavery.

Beloved centers on a former slave named Sethe. For years her home has been haunted by a spirit that Sethe believes is the ghost of her dead daughter. *Beloved* also explores the horrors of slavery through Sethe's memory and the memories of other former salves.

Oprah Winfrey costarred with Danny Glover and others in the film version of Beloved.

In April 1988, Morrison's *Beloved* won the Pulitzer Prize for fiction. She said it was a great honor and was deeply pleased. At 57 years old, Morrison was recognized as one of America's great writers. Ten years later, in 1998, a movie version of *Beloved* was made. It starred Oprah Winfrey as Sethe.

Despite all the success, Morrison still had much writing, teaching, and lecturing to do. In 1989 she took a teaching position at Princeton University in New Jersey.

Jazz

In 1992 Morrison published her sixth novel and a book of essays. The novel, *Jazz,* is a story of people in the community of Harlem in New York City. The novel is set in the 1920s, and although the story centers around a death, it is really a story about hope and healing and survival.

Playing in the Dark: Whiteness and the **Literary** *Imagination* was also published in 1992. It is a book of three essays that Morrison originally wrote and read at Harvard University in 1990. The essays are about **racial** attitudes of early American authors such as Mark Twain. They show how important race was in many early literary works.

Happiness and sorrow

Very early one morning in 1993, Morrison got a telephone call bringing her very exciting news. She was going to receive the Nobel Prize in Literature. The Nobel Prize is considered by many to be the highest recognition of a writer's talent.

But the year was also a sad one for Morrison. Very soon after she was honored with the Nobel Prize, her mother died. Her

Toni Morrison appeared on the cover of Time *magazine in 1998.*

> ### In Her Own Words
> "I regard the fact that my house burned down after I won the Nobel Prize to be better than having my house burn down without having won the Nobel Prize. Most people's houses just burn down. Period."

brother George also died that year. And on Christmas Day, her home on the Hudson River was destroyed by fire. She was at work in Princeton at the time, and only her son Slade was at home. Slade escaped without harm, but Morrison's papers weren't so lucky. She had a number of handwritten manuscripts stored under her bed—including seven versions of *The Bluest Eye*. But what hurt her most of all was the loss of her family photos and documents.

Paradise

Through the years, especially after a new book was published, Morrison has often said she will not write another novel. But then, an idea seems to grow in her imagination, and she starts the writing process all over again. Such was the case with Morrison's novel *Paradise*, published in 1999.

Still writing

There was much anticipation in 2003 when the publication Morrison's novel *Love* was announced. *Love* is about the different ways people can love and hate each other. Critics generally praised the novel and it has been very popular with readers.

With her son Slade, Morrison has written a number of books for children, including *The Book of Mean People*, which lets kids know that it's all right to feel angry sometimes, and *The Big Box*, about how children need and deserve their freedom.

Toni Morrison is a major American writer, some say America's best. She took what she learned from her grandparents and what she came to understand about race in the United States and wove it into stories with messages we can all appreciate. She writes as if she is telling her story out loud. This is one way she honors her African-American heritage. But she writes for everyone, no matter what their race, because she hopes that by sharing each other's stories, we may reach a greater understanding of one another.

In Her Own Words

"There's a difference between writing for a living and writing for life. If you write for a living, you make enormous compromises, and you might not ever be able to uncompromise yourself. If you write for life, you'll work hard; you'll do it in a disciplined fashion; you'll do what's honest, not what pays. You'll be willing to say no when somebody wants to play games with your work. You'll be willing to not sell it. You'll have a very strong sense of your work."

Toni Morrison continues to write, teach, and lecture today.

Glossary

activist person who believes in taking forceful action for political purposes

civil rights rights of all United States citizens to fair and equal treatment under the law. The civil rights movement was the name given to the long fight to gain civil rights for African Americans.

culture knowledge, beliefs, and behavior of a group of people

desegregated to end by law the separation or isolation of members of a particular race

idol person who is greatly admired

injustice unfairness or violation of the rights of another

justice quality of being fair or just

literature written works having lasting interest and ideas.

literary relating to writers, writing, or literature.

lynch to put to death without legal authority

myth story that explains something; legend

opera musical stage production in which the story is sung

philosophy study of basic ideas about knowledge, truth, right and wrong

prejudice favoring or dislike of something for no good or fair reason

racism belief that people of different races are not as good or equal as others. A racist is a person who practices racism.

segregate to separate, by races for example

sharecropper farmer who works the land owned by another in return for a portion of the crop

thesis long essay that presents the results of a writer's research

undergraduate person enrolled in college who has not yet received his or her degree

Timeline

1931 Chloe Anthony Wofford is born on February 18.

1949 Chloe graduates from high school.

1953 Now known as Toni Wofford, Chloe graduates from Howard University.

1955 Toni receives her master's degree.

1957 Begins teaching at Howard University.

1958 Marries Harold Morrison.

1961 First son, Harold Ford, is born.

1964 Goes to Europe, separates from her husband, and returns to the United States. Her second son, Slade Kevin, is born.

1965 Morrison becomes an editor at Random House.

1967 Moves to New York City.

1970 *The Bluest Eye* is published under the name Toni Morrison.

1973 *Sula* is published.

1975 *Sula* is nominated for a National Book Award.

1976 Morrison agrees to teach at Yale University.

1981 Morrison appears on the cover of *Newsweek* magazine.

1985 Writes first play, *Dreaming Emmett*, and wins New York State Governor's Art Award.

1988 *Beloved* wins Pulitzer Prize for fiction.

1993 Morrison wins the Nobel Prize in Literature.

2003 Morrison publishes her novel *Love*.

Further Information

Further reading

Blashfield, Jan. *Toni Morrison.* Philadelphia: Chelsea House, 2001.

Haskins, Jim. *Toni Morrison: Magic of Words.* Brookfield, Conn.: Millbrook Press, 2001.

Jones, Amy. *Toni Morrison.* Chanhassen, Minn.: Child's World, 2001.

Morrison, Toni, and Slade Morrison. *The Book of Mean People.* New York: Hyperion Books, 2005.

Addresses

Toni Morrison
Creative Writing Program
Princeton University
195 Nassau St.
Princeton, NJ 08544

Go On Girl Book Club
National Headquarters
P.O. Box 3368
New York, NY 10185

Howard University
2400 Sixth Street, NW
Washington, D.C. 20059

Index

African Ameican culture 25, 28, 40, 42, 46

Beloved 52, 53, 54
Bluest Eye, The 35, 36, 37, 42, 57

Carmichael, Stokely 28, 29, 30
civil rights 26, 27, 28, 30, 34
Cornell University 23, 25

Dreaming Emmett 50, 51

Howard University 16, 17, 18, 19, 20, 22, 23, 25, 26, 28, 31

Jazz 55
Jones, LeRoi 28

Love 57

Morrison, Harold 28, 31
Morrison, Harold Ford 28, 31, 33, 39, 40, 43, 47
Morrison, Slade Kevin 31, 33, 39, 40, 43, 47, 57, 58

National Book Critics Circle award 5, 47
National Book Foundation Medal 5
National Council on the Arts 50

National Honor Society 16
Newsweek 49
New York State Governor's Art Award 50
Nobel Prize 5, 6, 55, 57

Paradise 57
Playing in the Dark: Whiteness and the Literary Imagination 55

Pulitzer Prize 5, 54

Random House 33, 34, 39, 42, 43, 47, 50

segregation 10, 12, 20, 22, 23, 26, 28, 30
sharecroppers 8, 9, 10, 14
slavery 9, 14, 20, 42, 45, 46, 53
Sula 38, 40, 42

Tar Baby 49
Texas Southern University 24, 25

Yale University 43, 44
Young, Andrew 28

OCT 5 2005

32⁸⁶